TALKING POINTS

Twenty assignments for GCSE English oral work

Jim Sweetman

Chief Examiner
for the Midland Examining Group
GCSE English syllabus

Mary Glasgow Publications

M·G·P

Jim Sweetman taught English at GCE 'O' and CSE level for fifteen years in Coventry and Warwickshire. He is Joint Chief Examiner for the Midland Examining Group GCSE English syllabus and has worked on staged assessment and profiling in English since 1984.

© 1987 Jim Sweetman

First published in 1987 by
Mary Glasgow Publications Ltd
Avenue House
131–133 Holland Park Avenue
London W11 4UT

Typeset by Cambrian Typesetters,
Frimley, Surrey
Printed in Great Britain by
G. P. Printers, South Molton, Devon.

Illustrations by Phillip Burrows
Design by Penny Mills

ISBN 1 85234 069 X
Teacher's guide ISBN 1 85234 070 3

British Library Cataloguing in Publication Data
Sweetman, Jim.
    Talking points: twenty assignments for
    GCSE English oral work.
    1. English language—Spoken English
    I. Title
    428.3   PE1112
    ISBN 1–85234–069–X

Information about other MGP publications for English is available from Mary Glasgow Publications Ltd, Brookhampton Lane, Kineton, Warwick, CV35 0JB. Tel. (0926) 640 606.

CONTENTS

INTRODUCTION 4
WHY TALK?   THE VARIETIES OF TALK

USING THE ASSIGNMENTS 7

ASSIGNMENTS

This workbook is concerned with oral communication – the way in which people talk and listen to one another. Of course, talking and listening is something which we can all do from a very early age. But we may not be as good at it as we think we are.

How often have you said any of these (or had them said to you)?

WHY TALK?

Most murders take place in the home and the victims normally know their killers! Industrial disputes and strikes often seem to happen over trivial, unimportant things. How often do we hear people say things like 'If only they would sit down and talk about it'? It's very common for young people to feel that they have difficulty in talking with their parents. Perhaps they have a special friendship with a grandparent or another relative because these people have the time to talk and listen to them. A happy home is one where people talk a lot about their problems, about what they are doing or even about very little. Chatting and sharing our experiences is important in making us feel that we are valued and that we are somebody in the world.

But talk is even more important than this. It is the best way in which we can develop our ideas, change our opinions, look at difficulties in a new light and find solutions to problems. For these kinds of activity, talking is better than writing because what is said can be adjusted and modified while a discussion proceeds.

Imagine a group of people trying to plan and write a video to help sell a new record. They don't have the time to write each other letters about what their ideas are. So instead they get together and have a 'brainstorming' session where they put forward whatever ideas they have in whatever order the ideas occur to them. Someone has an idea. Another person might know exactly why it couldn't work but suggests a slightly different approach. Then someone else might remember a time when that was done somewhere else, and that somebody is an expert on it, and then it turns out that the first person knows her anyway. And so it goes on. Imagine how many letters that would take! It's exciting to use talk like this. If you've ever sat down with your friends and planned a day out or a party, then you'll know the feeling.

This book is about learning to talk more successfully, to communicate exactly what you want to say and to share your ideas and opinions. It allows you to practise talking in various ways and in different situations.

TALKING POINTS also offers you the chance to consider your own performance – to ask yourself just how good a talker and listener you are. Talking is a sharing experience. You could start by discussing how to be a better talker and what makes a good listener.

Finally, the GCSE examination recognises just how important talking and listening are. It encourages discussion in all your school subjects and actually gives a grade for your performance in English. Using this book you can demonstrate all the skills the examiner is looking for and note for yourself, with the help of your teacher, when they have been achieved.

THE VARIETIES OF TALK

We all need to talk and it would be a funny world if we didn't. But we may not realise just how many different kinds of talk we use in the course of a single week. Where will you be in ten years' time? What kind of talk will you be producing in your daily life? Sarah and Mark Wordsworth are in their mid twenties. Mark is a supervisor with a manufacturing firm and Sarah runs a small hairdressing business. What kind of talk do they need to use? Here's a typical diary for one week.

MONDAY

When Mark gets to work, there has been a mix-up over a delivery which should have been sent out on Friday. The customer is angry. Mark has to speak to the customer and calm him down. Then he has to find out what has gone wrong by talking to the shift foreman. The foreman blames the packers who parcel up the goods, so Mark has to talk to two of them. They blame the foreman. One of them becomes very upset and threatens to leave. Mark decides the foreman should take responsibility. He has to tell him that he has made a serious mistake which could cost the company orders.

Meanwhile, Sarah is talking to customers about all kinds of things. One of the customers says she thinks football hooligans and teenage glue-sniffers should be caned in public. Another customer starts to argue. Sarah manages to change the subject.

INTRODUCTION

TUESDAY——————————————

At the salon, the water pump breaks down. Sarah has to ring the repair man. He wants to know exactly what is not working and what caused the pump to stop. He says that he will not be able to come until Friday. Sarah has to persuade him to come first thing the following morning because without the pump her business cannot operate.

WEDNESDAY——————————————

Mark is interviewed for a promotion within the company. He has to sell himself and his skills to the Managing Director. He is on his own in front of five senior people for over an hour. The repair man arrives at the salon. He tries to sell Sarah a new pump. She refuses politely. Mark gets the job. He is really excited. On the way home he drives through a red traffic light without noticing. The police are there. He apologises. They tick him off and give him a caution this time. That evening Sarah and Mark have a row about who forgot to unplug the iron, but they soon make it up.

THURSDAY——————————————

Mark meets the staff who will work for him in his new job. He has to tell them what he expects from them – for example, that they should be at work on time every morning and report machine faults promptly. He has to be careful how he says it because they are people who were previously on the same level as him. Sarah has a trainee starting on work-experience from the local school. She has to explain to her how to wash the customers' hair without straining their necks or getting shampoo in their eyes and how to choose the best conditioner for each customer. That evening she and Mark sit down to work out her VAT returns for the month. They work together through all her receipts for the month because the books do not balance.

FRIDAY——————————————

The woman who used to have Mark's new job retires. The Managing Director is taken ill and Mark is given ten minutes to make up a short speech thanking her for all her efforts. Sarah telephones her orders through to the wholesaler for the following week.

SATURDAY——————————————

Mark decides to buy a new car with his increased salary. The salesman is fast-talking and persuasive. Mark has to keep his cool and not be rushed. He talks it over with Sarah at home. She makes some telephone calls and finds the same model £500 cheaper at another garage.

And so it goes on. That is just one week. Mark and Sarah are always talking and for many different purposes. They must be good talkers to be where they are. After all, Mark could have lost his temper on Monday and been left without staff if he had acted hastily. That might have lost him his new job and the car.

Sarah might have had to close the salon for a week if the water pump had not been mended immediately. The argument on Wednesday might have ended in divorce! Sarah and Mark could have ended the week separate and broke if they had not been able to talk their way through their problems.

USING THE ASSIGNMENTS

There are twenty different assignments in this book which cover a wide variety of talking and listening situations. It is very useful to be able to work as a member of a group. It is equally important to be able to speak out on your own or to lead a discussion.

Your teacher will provide you with an *Oracy profile* which indicates what you might have achieved on completion of each assignment. With your teacher and classmates, it is important to consider whether or not you have really managed to learn the skills set out there and to what extent you could do the same again in a slightly different situation.

As you work through the workbook, you will become better at knowing your strengths and weaknesses. You may realise, for example, that you talk too much and interrupt others.

Or perhaps you tend to lose the thread of what is going on and say things which do not make sense. The next time you work on an assignment, you can pay attention to that particular point and correct it. The others in your group can help as well, by telling you if you go wrong and by making sure you take an active part.

For many of the assignments you will have to work in pairs and groups, often with people you do not normally work with. For most discussions, mixed groups of boys and girls are much more natural. You are quite likely to find some of the things you are asked to do a little embarrassing. Don't worry. Everyone feels the same and if, in the end, you become a more confident talker, that will be an asset to you throughout your life.

ZOO

THE PROBLEM

The local Zoo is overcrowded already. Now they have been offered a pair of dolphins to add to their other animals. One of the existing animal enclosures will have to be converted into a dolphinarium and the Zoo owners have decided to take the opportunity to re-house all the animals. It is up to your group to recommend where the animals should now be housed. You have a plan of the Zoo and some notes about the various animals to help you in this.

Spend a session talking about this. You will need about 20–30 minutes. Sit in a circle or around a table.

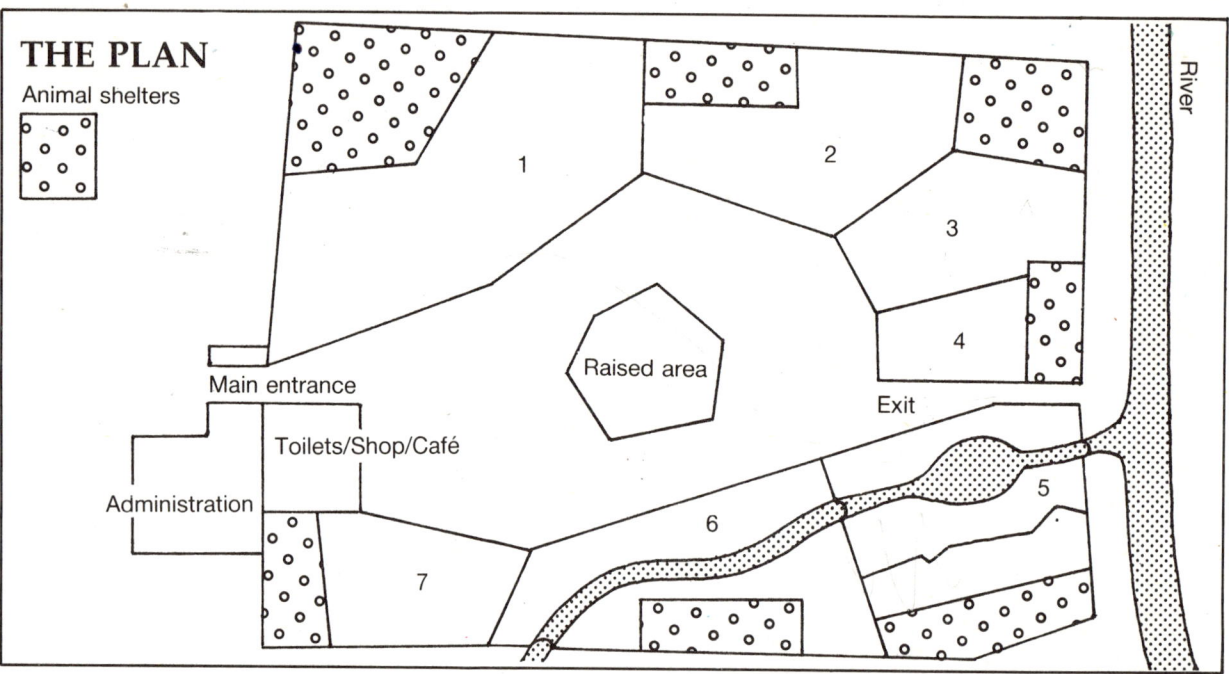

THE PLAN

Animal shelters

1   2   3   4

River

Raised area

Main entrance

Toilets/Shop/Café

Administration

Exit

5   6   7

THE ANIMALS

Monkeys: Noisy. Will tease birds. Very scared of lions.

Lions and Tigers: Quite easily upset. Need peace and quiet. Very strong-smelling which may upset some people. Need to be away from animals which they might want to attack or they can behave very viciously. Popular with the visitors.

Elephants: Need plenty of space. Should be well away from lions whose presence upsets them. Their food is very bulky and large quantities are required.

Penguins: Need flowing water.

Polar bears: Need water. Will eat penguins.

Antelopes and Zebra: Need grazing space. Rather timid and easily startled.

Tropical birds: Very noisy. Popular with visitors.

TALKBACK

How did you do? Use this checklist to grade your own performance. Just pick out and write down the five comments which best describe your contribution to the session.

★ *Interrupted others in the group*

★ *Made jokes and funny comments*

★ *Didn't listen to others*

★ *Said something which took the discussion forward*

★ *Started the discussion on a new point after it had stopped*

★ *Noticed and mentioned something the group had missed*

★ *Spoke my mind*

★ *Was really involved*

★ *Was rude about what someone in the group had to say*

★ *Was willing to change my mind*

★ *Supported my friends*

★ *Went off the subject*

★ *Listened to what others said and replied to it*

★ *Didn't say much*

★ *Insulted someone*

★ *Lost interest as the discussion went on*

★ *Kept putting forward the same solution*

★ *Got angry with others in the group*

Now pick out for another member of the group the five statements which describe their contribution best. Compare your results. Are you the talker that you thought you were?

SCHOOL FUND

Your school sponsored walk has raised £3,000 and a PTA jumble sale has raised another £450. It has been decided that the pupils in the school should be given a chance to recommend how the money should be spent. The school has asked for suggestions as to what the money should be spent on and the following items were most popular.

THE TASK ▽

It is your group's task to consider these various suggestions and to decide which the school should support. Remember that you will be expected to justify and support the proposals which you put forward. The approximate cost of each item is given to help you decide.

★ *New computers for the computer room.* *£500 each*

★ *New noticeboards for the Entrance Hall.* *£150 each*

★ *Extensions to the tuck shop to allow an extra hatch to be open at breaktimes.* *£850*

★ *Bench seats in the playground.* *£125 each*

★ *Paperback fiction books for the School Library.* *£450*

★ *A powerful new microscope for the Science Department.* *£700*

★ *A contribution to the Minibus replacement fund.* *£?*

★ *A large word-processor for the General Office.* *£1,200*

★ *A video recorder and a camera for the English Department.* *£1,375*

★ *A grant to start a School Youth Club.* *£250*

★ *New curtains for the school stage.* *£650*
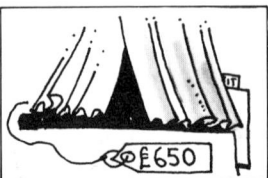

The total cost of these items could easily be £7,000 so your job is not an easy one. How will you set about it? Which of these approaches makes most sense to you?

1. Decide for yourself what the money should be spent on and then argue with the rest of the group so as to persuade them to agree.
2. Don't make any definite decisions yourself. Criticise what anyone else says and show them that their ideas are wrong.
3. Work through the list identifying the points in favour of and against each one.
4. Have a vote among yourselves to decide which items you want the money spent on.
5. Write down individual lists of how you would like the money spent and then compare them.
6. Decide what you would absolutely *not* want the money spent on and make sure that those items are rejected.

In this case many people would say that number three was the best and the fairest choice because it would give all the options a fair hearing. It might also be the most *effective* because, although it seems a long-winded way to do it, with the other ways your group might easily repeat itself. Have your discussion. Look back to the talkback checklist in Assignment 1 and decide as a group whether your talk this time was better than before. If so, try to say why.

Now appoint two people to present your group's conclusions. Brief them on what to say. They will need to make some notes!

NOTES.   SCHOOL FUND MEETING

24 September.

£600 Curtains ??   No

+£350 Computers — who uses them ?

+£150

£1100 so far   ■ Benches — all Support
■ Youth Club — ?
Find out more about it.

THE COMMITTEE

In the last assignment you decided which of the proposals for spending £3,450 of the school's money you wanted to support. That was quite a realistic task. Many schools now ask their students how school funds should be spent. If your school does not, it would be an excellent oral exercise (and good for your fellow pupils as well) to go and see your head teacher and ask him or her to change the system so that this happens!

This assignment is realistic for two of the group and less real for the others because they are asked to 'role-play' or pretend that they are someone else. (School classrooms don't contain many parents, grannies, policemen, careers officers or Martians but it is sometimes useful to pretend that they do.) In this assignment, the rest of the group will help the two main speakers by playing their parts as realistically as possible.

THE TASK ▽

Two of the group have to present the conclusions of the previous assignment to a meeting which is to decide how the money should finally be spent. They have to meet with some of the following people who will be acted by the rest of the group. If you are acting out one of these parts, ask yourself what you think this person would feel about the money and what kinds of projects they would support. Forget your own views and concentrate on 'being' this person for a while.

WHO'S WHO?

Councillor Jackson: Chairman of the School Governors. He/She could be a politician who remembers schools as bare, empty buildings with very few facilities or, on the other hand, he/she might have gone to a 'public' school where parents paid for their children's education. You decide, and, beginning from what you choose, start to build a picture of the councillor.

Mr or Mrs Walters: The Parent Teacher Association representative. Has two children: Eric is in the Sixth Form and Katie is in the Second Year. Has been on the PTA Committee for five years.

Mr or Mrs Grover: The head teacher. Be careful with this role. What would the head teacher really want? How would he or she set about getting his or her own way? You may need to be quite *subtle*.

Mr or Miss Wilson: The Head of P.E. and teacher representative on the Committee.

Mr or Mrs MacIntyre: Another School Governor, younger than all the others and with very go-ahead ideas.

You can add to this list if you like. You can even ask your teacher to join in! The Chairperson will have to work quite hard. He or she should look at Assignment 16 to check up on what has to be done!

Set a time for this discussion, maybe thirty minutes, so that you have time to discuss what happened afterwards. Did you manage to make it seem real for the two who presented the proposals? Was it easier or more difficult for them in this situation? Did you manage to play your role realistically throughout the exercise? Who in the group kept up their act best?

Sometimes it can help if you tape a task like this. It makes the people playing a role be more conscious of what they are saying. You could also ask another group to watch and to make their own assessments using the *Oracy checklist* profile from your teacher.

DE/IGNING THE EXTEN/ION

The Peters family (Andy, Helen and their two sons, Duane and Tom) live in a detached house on the main road out of the town. It is a nice house but quite small. Now Helen's mother is growing old and they feel that they should have her to live with them. She has some money from the sale of her house which they have decided to use to extend their home. They have come to a firm of architects for ideas on how this should be done.

THE TASK ▽

It is your group's task to look at the plans of the house and the needs of the family and decide how best to design an extension. You do not have to come up with a single plan, but whatever you suggest, you must be prepared to back this up with your reasoning.

This is the way architects often work, discussing ideas amongst themselves before they start a design. That way problems can be ironed out at an early stage and all the possible options can be looked at closely. But it is worth remembering that architects are busy people. They charge a lot of money for their time. Their talk has to aim to solve the problems effectively in the shortest possible time.

The Peters' house and garden is shown on the plan. One of the partners from the firm of architects has visited them and made some notes which are also printed for you. One of your group might like to play this part and to read these notes back to the group before you start talking.

THE PLAN

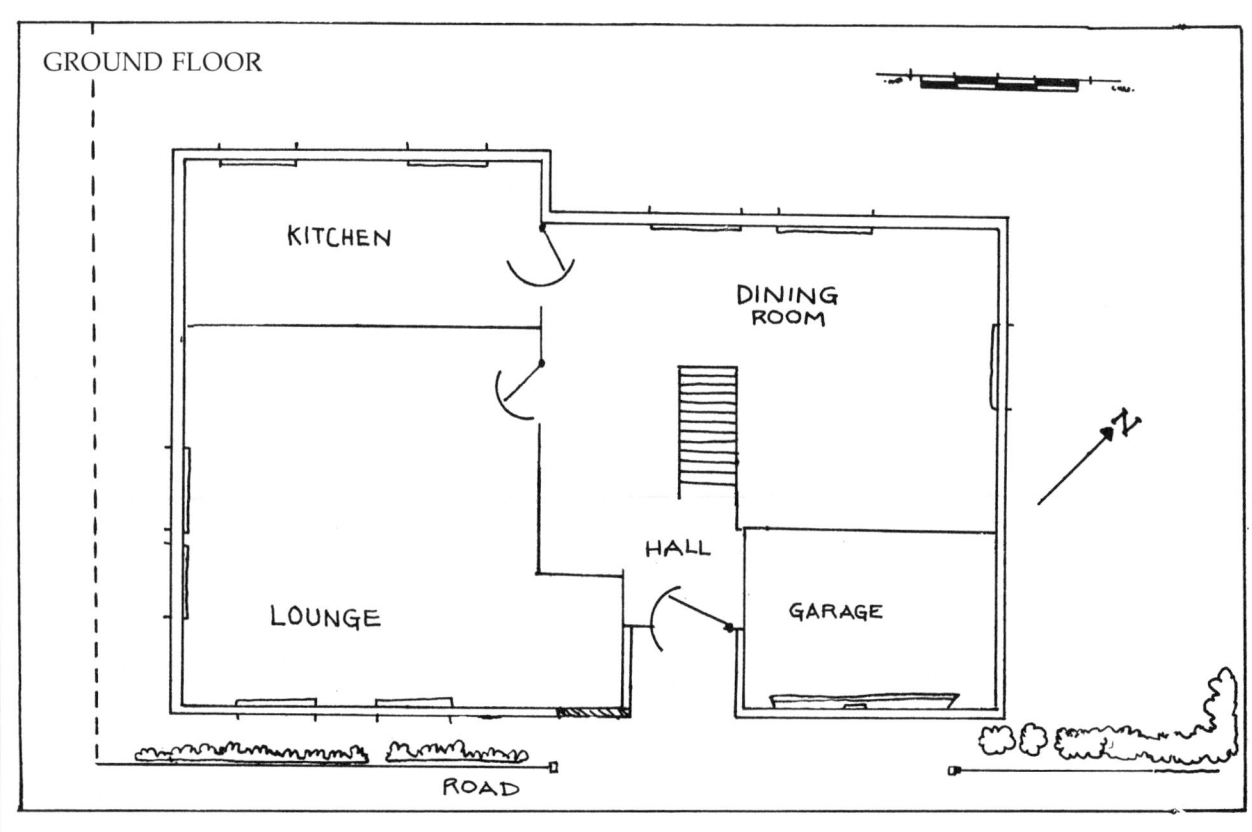

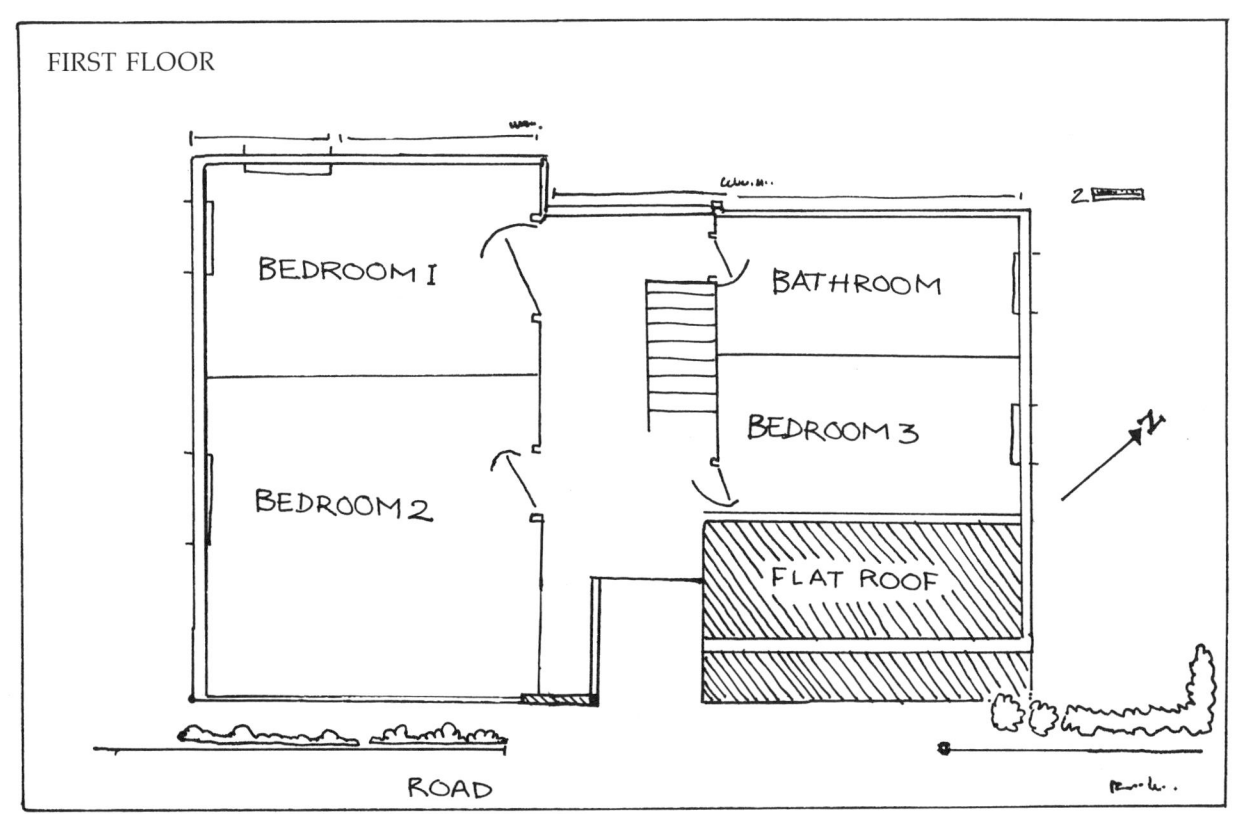

FIRST FLOOR

BEDROOM 1

BEDROOM 2

BATHROOM

BEDROOM 3

FLAT ROOF

ROAD

Notes:

Mrs Peters' mother is an old lady. She needs to be close to the bathroom if possible. She does not like noise and should be as far away from the boys as possible. Duane has his own stereo in his room.

The family would quite like to extend the dining room at some time or perhaps have a conservatory on the side of the house.

The garage is full of junk. The family leave their car in the road.

Mrs Peters says that the kitchen is too small and that the hall is too large.

The main road is very busy and is separated from the house by a thick hedge.

When you finish, draw a plan of your favourite proposal. Write a letter to Mr and Mrs Peters to go with it, explaining why you have chosen to suggest that the work should be carried out in this way.

Time left? Improvise, with role-play, a meeting between Mr and Mrs Peters and the architects. The architects explain to the Peters what is involved.

Or, with your group, think about how your school was planned. Are there problem areas where the design could be improved? Could the rooms be better used?

POCKET MONEY

Have you ever asked for more pocket money? No, of course not! But you might know people who have. This assignment is for you to decide how much pocket money is fair. You could talk about pocket money by working out how much you need to live on for a week or how much you would like, but that might not be very realistic.

This assignment looks at the household budget from another direction and begins from the family income. It means that when you talk you begin with some hard facts. Most real talk is like this. It has a real content. You don't argue with your parents about pocket money in general. You ask for £2 when you are getting £1.50 and if you only get 50p you ask for £1!

THE BROWN'S BUDGET

Mr Brown is a horizontal borer in an engineering works. Mrs Brown is a part-time receptionist. Tracey (18 years) works in an office on a YTS course. Winston (15) has a paper round. Amelia (12) and Carlton (5) don't earn anything.

WHAT THEY EARN	
Mr Brown's salary	£12,000 a year
Mrs Brown's salary	£6,250 a year
Tracey Brown's salary	£25 per week
Winston Brown's paper round	£10 per week
Family allowances	£28 per week

WHAT THEY SPEND	
Income tax and National Insurance	£2,000 a year
Rent and rates	£3,200 a year
Car	£1,750 a year
Food	£3,800 a year
Holidays	£1,500 a year
TV/Video rent and licence	£350 a year
Furniture/ Appliances/Things for home	£1,000 a year
Decorating	£500 a year
Going out	£1,000 a year
Clothes	£750 a year

They try to save as well, so this doesn't leave much. Perhaps you think they could cut down in certain areas.

THE TASK

Your problem is to decide how much pocket money you think the children should get. Should Tracey get any at all? Maybe she should pay her parents something? What should the younger children get? Should they all get the same? Should Winston get as much as Tracey? Discuss this with your partner/ group.

Come up with some firm figures and some reasons for your decisions. If you have time, compare the Browns' situation with your own. How much do you get and how do you spend it?

SCHOOL UNIFORM 1 discussion/persuasion

Ashby School and Hampton School are to merge because of their falling numbers of pupils. Although the schools have much in common and are both comprehensives, they make very different demands on their pupils in terms of uniform.

Here are the schools' uniform lists. All pupils are expected to conform to these until they leave in the Fifth Year.

ASHBY SCHOOL

Boys
Black blazer
Black or brown leather shoes
Grey trousers
Grey or white shirt
Dark blue and silver tie

Girls
Black blazer
Plain grey skirt
Black well-fitting shoes
Grey or blue socks
Blue open-necked shirt

HAMPTON SCHOOL

Boys and Girls

Red or black sweater with round or V-shaped neck
Red, black or white shirt
Suitable trousers or skirt
Trainers or denim jeans may not be worn.

THE TASK ▽

The schools have a problem. What uniform should they adopt in the future? Your group has been asked to make suggestions. Spend some time discussing the alternatives. You might like to talk about which of these uniforms is most like the one worn at your school or, if your school does not have a uniform, which of these you would prefer.

Here are one school's reasons for wearing a school uniform:
1. It shows that a pupil will accept the aims and fellowship of the school.
2. It indicates that parents will co-operate with the school and support its aims.
3. It sets a standard of dress which indicates to the general public the quality of the school.
4. It stimulates pride in personal appearance and the appearance of the school as a whole.
5. It aids good manners, as well-dressed pupils are generally polite.
6. It reminds the wearer of the school code of behaviour.
7. It has a great value on school journeys and visits.
8. It offers all pupils a fair chance to attain equality of dress whatever the financial circumstances of the parents.

NOW ARGUE YOUR CASE

In talking about these two schools' uniforms, you have probably found yourself saying that you prefer one to the other. The next stage of the discussion is to argue *for* one of the uniforms and *against* the other one. In your group, try to persuade each other to decide in favour of one of the uniforms. You will need to think of some real arguments to support your case.

Have you considered these points?
How much will it cost?
How long will it last?
Will it stay looking neat?
Will the pupils look smart?
Will it be popular or disliked? By pupils?
   By parents?

Remember that you are trying to *persuade* and that you persuade people by how well you put forward your point of view. If you shout and interrupt, you will never win a real argument. If you do not listen to the points which others make, then you will never be able to explain why they are wrong! So give your reasons carefully and listen to what the others have to say. You may find some of the reasons they give can support your own argument too, when seen from another point of view.

OPPOSED TO UNIFORM?

You could be opposed to all uniform. If so, broaden out the discussion to put your point of view.

SCHOOL UNIFORM 2 devising a survey

The last assignment encouraged you to discuss school uniform. In this assignment, you are encouraged to talk to other people about school uniform and to find out their views.

There are two ways to find out what people think. One is to talk to them, probably in the form of an interview. The other is to ask them to fill in some kind of form or questionnaire. If you want to find out about opinions generally rather than about what a particular person thinks, then a survey is probably the best way.

WHAT DOES A SURVEY INVOLVE?

There are at least three stages, only one of which is going out asking questions!

STAGE ONE is deciding what to ask. What are the questions which will tell you what you want to know? How should you phrase questions to make sure that you find out the information you want?

STAGE TWO is giving out the survey. Who do you want to fill the forms in? If you give the forms just to your friends, you will probably find that their views are very like yours. If you give the forms just to adults, they may think quite differently from you. Most surveys try to use a mixed group or sample so as to find out what people think generally.

STAGE THREE is analysing the results. If you ask ten people fifty questions and each question can have five answers, then you could have 2,500 columns (and take up a few spare days) to compare the answers! A good survey asks a few well-chosen questions and produces answers (or data) which can easily be analysed.

PLANNING THE QUESTIONS

The aim of this session is to produce a questionnaire made up of a series of questions which you can ask people.

Look at these two questions. Which will provide answers that will be easier to analyse?

Question 1: *What do you think should be the main colour of the school uniform?*

Question 2: *If you are in favour of school uniform, ring the colour which you would like as the main colour*

BLACK	GREEN
BROWN	RED
BLUE	OTHER

The answer of course is the second question. It takes away a little choice from the person who fills it in but it saves you from having to work out whether an answer like indigo' means blue or not!

Other easy-to-answer questions are those with YES/NO answers: *Should jeans be allowed? Should trainers be worn?* Of course some people who think that clean trainers are all right but not dirty ones, will have problems, but when you analyse the results you will be able to see what percentage of the people surveyed were, broadly speaking, in favour of trainers. That is probably the important point.

1

Now BRAINSTORM the issue. Talk about uniform. What items of clothing should be included and asked about? What will there be most disagreement about? Are you going to include jewellery, make-up or hair styles?

2

Start making a note of questions. At this stage think of as many questions as you can. Make sure someone is writing them down.

4

Try them on your friends to make sure they make sense or that you haven't left out some obvious alternatives which you should have included.

3

Sort out the questions. Work in pairs, or singly, on tidying them up. Remember to make them easy to analyse like the examples on page 20.

5

Try to end up with maybe ten or fifteen questions which you can ask. Work out how you are going to record your results. Ticks in columns is one good way.

6

Decide what details you are going to need to know about the people you interview. Most adults dislike telling younger people their age but they might admit to being 'over 20', 'over 30' or 'over 40'. You might ask pupils which year they are in within the school and that will be more useful information than which class they are in. It might be interesting to know whether the adults in your survey had to wear uniform when they were at school.

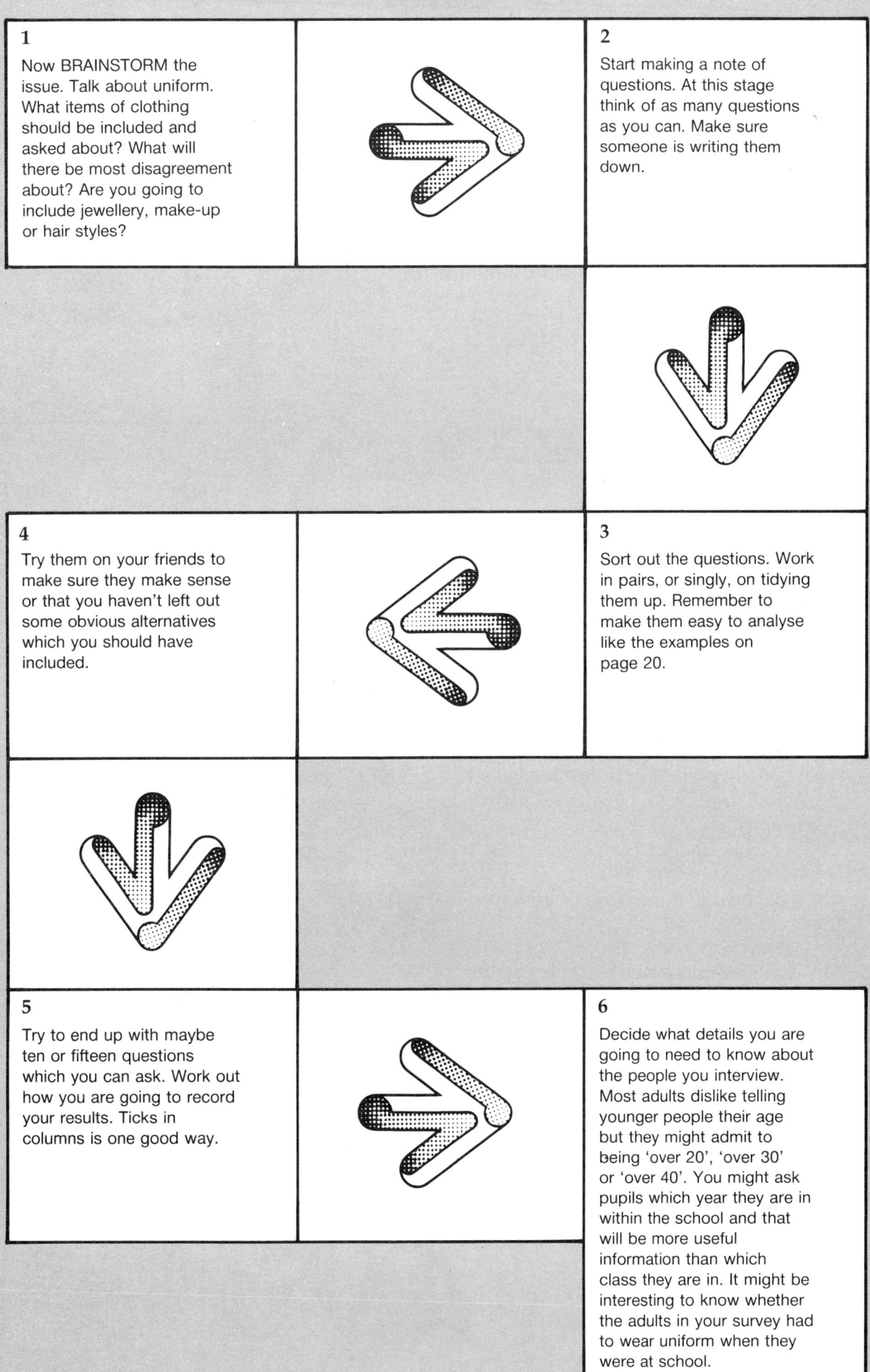

SCHOOL UNIFORM 3 carrying out a survey

This is not as easy as you may think. You will need clipboards and pencils. Practise holding them, writing and talking at the same time. Carry out your first survey in school at a breaktime and then you might just be ready to try the teachers or the outside world!

REMEMBER THESE TIPS FOR GOOD RESULTS

1. Survey in pairs, never crowd round people and NEVER knock on strange doors. Shopping centres or outside the local post-office are ideal places.

2. Approach people briskly and politely. Practise saying something like this: 'Excuse me, I am a Fifth-Year pupil at . . . . . . School and I have to complete a survey of public opinion as part of my GCSE course. I wonder if you would mind answering one or two questions.' If they look uncertain, reassure them: 'They are about school uniform and it will only take a minute or two.' Look interested in what they have to say. When you finish, be sure to thank them.

3. Try to find a variety of people to ask so that you have men and women of different ages.

4. Always look serious and sensible. If you take your survey seriously, so will the people you stop. Always be polite even if people are quite rude to you. There are people who dislike being approached in the street and you should respect their views.

5. Keep your answers neatly so that you can read them when you get back to school.

1

2

3

4

5

∫CHOOL UNIFORM 4 analysing results

ANALYSING THE RESULTS

The more replies obtained by a survey, the more reliable and trustworthy are its results. You should aim to ask at least fifty people for their views and up to a hundred would be better. Now you can see why it was important to ask simple questions!

Analysing the results will involve some careful counting and eventually you should try to end up with percentages in your results. An easy way to do this is to begin by looking at the questionnaires and sorting some out so as to ensure that you have a balanced sample (the same number of males and females and a range of ages). You might well find that you had asked a lot more women than men to answer your questions or that you had asked a lot of elderly people because they had more time to stand and talk to you. If you end up with 50 or 100 questionnaires to analyse, working out percentages will be easy.

PRESENTING YOUR FINDINGS

If this book were about writing, it would make sense to write up your results as a report – that is, an account of what you have found out and some comment on it, perhaps to say what was surprising or unusual. However, in the real world, surveys are often reported at press conferences where journalists are invited to ask questions and to hear about what you have discovered.

PRESENTING INFORMATION

At your press conference, you must make your presentation briefly, clearly and visually. Graphs and diagrams may help to show the results well. You will also have to order what you have to say so that your important findings are emphasised. Aim to spend ten minutes or less on presenting your information and allow time for questions afterwards. Another group can act as the journalists and it will then be their task to write an article which describes your findings. How well you have presented the information will be clear from what they write!

THE INTERVIEW

Anyone who watches breakfast television, documentaries or news broadcasts will have seen interviews taking place. Sometimes these programmes are called 'chat shows', as if people just natter away to one another for twenty minutes or so. In fact, interviewing is a very skilled craft whether you are a journalist trying to make a cunning politician admit to something he or she would rather not talk about or a chat show host trying to make a boring old film star say something interesting!

Here are some of the things good interviewers do. The best way to see them in action is to watch a few videos or television programmes and to try to spot them as they occur.

Good interviewers

★ *Put their subject at ease. Say things to help them relax.*

★ *Always look interested in what the subject has to say. They may nod or make 'mm' noises as they speak or use 'body language', perhaps by leaning slightly towards the interviewee.*

★ *Know when to interrupt – without seeming rude – if the interview is not going very well.*

★ *Can 'steer' the conversation to a new and interesting subject.*

★ *Can bring an interview to an end without seeming to finish abruptly.*

★ *Find something out about their subject before the interview starts.*

★ *Make sure that there are no long pauses during the interview.*

★ *Set the 'tone' of the interview. Is it serious or light? Incidentally, good interviewers never laugh at their own jokes!*

INTERVIEW OR INTERROGATION?

Classroom interviews often seem like a police interrogation rather than a pleasant interview. The idea of these two tasks is not to find out someone's secrets but to encourage them to talk about themselves or some aspect of their lives. Remember that the purpose of a 'chat show' interview is firstly to entertain the audience – this is more important than the information you gain.

THE FIRST TASK

Interview another member of the class about his or her spare-time occupations. This should obviously not be someone you go around with yourself.

Talk to your subject briefly *before* the interview and make the interview itself last five minutes EXACTLY.

Using the checklist on page 24, get the rest of your group to discuss your performance. Which of those skills did you show? If you can video your performance or make a tape recording of it, this will help you to see what they mean.

THE SECOND TASK

Interview an adult – a teacher or a relative, perhaps. Decide with your subject, before you start, what the interview is broadly going to be about – leisure interests, sporting or musical preferences, views about current issues are all good starting points. Try to work to a set time so that the interview does not become long and boring. If you work on this at home, it is a good idea not to interview your immediate family. You know your parents, brothers and sisters far too well for an interview with them to sound genuine because you already know the answers they will give. But if you talk to an uncle or aunt, a friend of your parents or a neighbour, then you will certainly find out something new.

You will soon find that the questions you ask, how you express them and the ways in which you let the interview develop, are all important qualities. However exciting or boring your subject is, the way you do the interview will make a considerable difference to its interest value.

Having practised interview technique in this assignment, watch out for chances to put what you have learned to good use. Coursework in other subjects may be helped by interviews with people about your projects and practical work. If your school has a school magazine, you could arrange to do an interview for it – perhaps with a speaker who visits the school to give a talk (even if the talk is not for your year).

MAKING SPEECHES

Speaking in public can be an ordeal for everyone, young or old. There are even many teachers who will not speak in public meetings although they have a lot to say in the classroom! If you feel nervous about having to speak in public, even if it is only to your own class, don't be surprised. Most people feel exactly as you do.

This assignment aims to help you over your fears by showing you how to plan carefully and by giving you something specific to talk about. For some people, of course, a five-minute talk is child's play. But for most of us, it is hard work. What matters is having the confidence to speak out – plenty of adequate preparation can help with this. The big question many people ask at this stage is 'Should I write out the whole speech?' If you do that, it will probably sound flat and dull when you read it. Some people manage well with a few scribbled notes on a scrap of paper or card – but this method can leave others struggling to read their own handwriting to find what they were going to say next!

Politicians often have their speeches written out for them. The text of what they are going to say is sometimes released to the newspapers before they have said it! They are sometimes trained by professional people to speak out loudly and know a few old tricks. For example, politicians often say things in groups of three for maximum effect. Try reading this out loud (it might help if you imitate a politician!).

> 'We need to start taking environmental issues very seriously, as we promised in our manifesto . . .'

Then try this:

> 'The people of this country want to be able to drink clean water, to breathe clean air and to bring up their children in a clean environment!'

This device is known as the 'rule of three' and can help a speaker to sound convincing by reinforcing the point. At a big meeting, a politician sometimes stops between each point of emphasis for some applause. Look at how the language of the second speech is also more *emotive*. You really feel something must be dirty even if you're not quite sure what it is! Every year politicians of all persuasions hold conferences to discuss their policies. Try to watch some of these critically, not so much listening to what the speechmaker says, but to the way in which he or she says it. Watch out for:

An emotional appeal –

'And today I ask you to think of those in hardship who cannot even afford their TV licence . . . I call on the Government to consider the plight of . . .'

Attempts to involve the audience –

'Well, comrades . . . Fellow delegates . . . My friends . . .'

Speaking very personally to an audience –

'And you know, really and truly, that I am a housewife as well and we all understand, don't we, how difficult it can be to make ends meet . . . But you see, the country is just like a big shop. If we give away the sweets today, how can we buy more to sell tomorrow?'

'How would you like it if the police stopped you every time you went for a walk and searched you on the pavement?'

'Those who have the most money, the rich and the wealthy must play a part in rebuilding this country.'

Saying things more than once for emphasis –

A rhetorical question (that's one to which you already know the answer, so you ask it just for effect) –

You can pick up some ideas from watching politicians, but there is no need to feel that you should make a political speech when you are giving a talk about your budgie! Here are some more general points to bear in mind:

★ *Greet your audience.*

★ *Try to keep eye contact with them. Look up, not down. Pulling your hair back from your face before you start will help to give the impression that you are looking up even if you are not!*

★ *Keep notes simple. Use them as cues to remind you of the order of what you want to say.*

THE TASK ▽

Try at least one of the following:

1. Watch a recording of a politician making a speech several times. See how the features mentioned above occur. What other things do you notice? How does the politician use 'body language' to help to underline a point?

2. Make up some silly political speeches. What you say can be ridiculous but make the speeches sound genuine by using the tricks mentioned. Tape them to see afterwards how convincing you were.

3. Make a serious speech on a subject which you are concerned about and bear these ideas in mind if you are speaking in a debate.

MAKING A POINT

Here is a speech about whether fox-hunting should be banned. It is part of a school debate. Try to read it out loud in a convincing way. Alongside it are some comments about how the speech sets out to gain the listener's sympathy.

'Ladies and Gentlemen.

It is my task today to persuade you that the hunting down and slaughter of dumb animals which some people are misguided enough to think of as a sport should be stopped immediately.

I want to begin by asking you to think of two pictures in your mind. The first is of a small creature, perhaps a little larger than your cat but probably smaller than your dog. Like them, it is furry with big attractive eyes but it is also secretive and timid. It prefers the countryside to the town, where it can run wild and free and rear its cubs in sunny woodland glades. It avoids human contact because it is so timid but occasionally we may be lucky enough to catch a glimpse of a bushy tail or to see the cubs frolicking and playing outside the earth. It is of course the fox, ladies and gentlemen, of which I speak.

Now picture something else, much larger than the tiny fox and with a bulging paunch spilling out of its red suit. It is red-faced to match from too much whisky the night before and its eyes are slitty, pig-like and half-closed. It might be dribbling a little from the exercise of running a few feet from the Range Rover to get onto its horse. It has a whip in one hand to beat the horse and a glass in the other. It hopes to find a fox, chase it for miles and block up its home so that it cannot escape. Then, when the fox falls exhausted it will watch vicious dogs tear it to pieces until it dies. It may smear the blood from this revolting escapade onto the faces of its children as part of an old tradition.

Well, ladies and gentlemen, whose side are you on?'

always be polite to the audience ...

... tell the audience where you're going!

...build a picture in their minds. Little 'cats' and 'dogs' – we all love them!

aaah!

... refer back to the audience. Keep them involved!

...bring in a contrast

...rule of three! (page 26)

... make the hunter unsympathetic ...

...and inhuman

... more savage than the fox ...

... end with a rhetorical question!

What sort of notes would help you give a
similar talk? They might look something like
this.

L and G.

1. _It is my task today_ ...
which some people ...   dumb animals
immediately.   should be stopped

2. _Fox_ ...   I want to begin by asking you ...
think of cat and dog → furry, attractive,
timid. Playing with cubs.

3. Hunter ... much larger, fat. Red faced from
too much whisky the night before ... eyes
slitty, _pig-like_ and _half-closed_. Range Rover.
Run to horse.

4. Well, L & G, whose side are you on ?

THE TASK ▽

Make a similar kind of speech on one of the
following subjects. Use the same framework.
Greet your audience and involve them as you
talk. Try to create pictures in their minds of
what you are trying to get across to them.
Don't worry too much about your own
opinions here. It is how you say it, rather than
what you say, which is important.

★   Animal vivisection

★   Whaling

★   Bull-fighting

THE CLASS TALK

In many ways, giving a talk to your friends is worse than talking to an audience you do not know. But it is something which you will be pleased to have achieved. This is a long assignment, but the short talk you give can form a major part of your oral assessment, so it is important to get it right!

CHOOSING YOUR SUBJECT

Talk about something which you:

a. are interested in.
b. are actively involved in or have had something to do with in the past.
c. enjoy.
d. are often involved with adults in doing.
e. have strong views or convictions about.

Think about these suggestions:

An interesting holiday
    Somewhere foreign
    A school trip
    Going off on my own
    An adventure holiday
    A working holiday

My spare-time hobby
    Fishing
    Sport
    Music
    Collecting
    Cycling
    Cooking
    Motor bikes
    Dress-making

My part-time job
    Baby-sitting
    Paper round
    In the cafe
    At the shop

My past
    Where I used to live
    Old relatives
    Where my family came from

My views
    Nuclear weapons/Nuclear power
    Politics
    The World today
    Abortion
    Marriage and relationships
    Drugs
    Contraception and the young
    Rock groups and music
    Fashions

You can hardly say now, 'I don't know what to talk about . . .'! Your problem will be choosing. Use the list of hints at the start of the assignment to help you decide.

PLANNING WHAT TO SAY

Make notes about what you are going to say but *don't scribble them* so that they cannot be read. Try writing the first few words of a sentence, and remembering what you want to follow them with, rather than writing it all out. If you feel that you must write it out, use a highlighting pen or a pale felt-tip to pick out the beginning of each point or sentence. Use cards to make notes on or small sheets of paper – a big sheaf of A4 paper is very distracting for an audience.

Use 'props' to help you. Photographs, posters, diagrams on the board, equipment, souvenirs or whatever will help you to get started and to hold your audience's attention.

ON THE DAY

– Make sure you are fully prepared. Get yourself in the right relaxed mood.

– Be interesting.

– If you make a mistake, don't panic. Apologise ('Excuse me while I just refer to my notes a moment') and then carry on.

– Use your hands to emphasise the points which you are making.

– Think before you answer questions. Be prepared to pause for a moment and to think about what you are going to say.

WHAT MAKES A GOOD TALK

The best talk is one which suits its purpose. If your hobby is fishing and you give a talk to the fishing club, it will be a different talk from the one you would give to your classmates or a group of younger children. If you are representing your workmates in a conflict over conditions at work, you will not talk in the same way as you would if you were giving a talk on your summer holiday in Majorca! However, there are some general points which we can apply to a classroom talk. When you say at the end 'That was interesting!' or 'I enjoyed that', it is likely that these are exactly the points you are taking into account.

─── *The content* ───

★ *I could understand clearly what was described or discussed.*

★ *I could follow the argument put forward and see where the talk was 'going'.*

★ *The speaker knew what he or she was talking about.*

★ *I didn't feel that I was being lectured at or that the speaker lacked any confidence in what he or she was saying.*

★ *Questions were answered in a full and interesting way.*

─── *The delivery* ───

★ *The talk was well paced and clear.*

★ *The speaker kept up eye contact and tried to involve the audience.*

★ *The speaker used gestures effectively and appeared relaxed.*

★ *The speaker did not read a prepared speech or lose his/her way in a sheaf of scribbled notes.*

When you give your talk, bear these points in mind. You will find that, as you get under way, your confidence will increase and the words flow easily.

GIVING DIRECTIONS

Talk is at its most useful when we are giving directions or instructions. Think of the difference between a cookery lesson at school and reading a recipe book. Written instructions and directions are often difficult to follow and often downright misleading. Do you have a computer at home with a supposedly 'easy-to-follow' manual? Have you ever built a kit from instructions or tried to follow a dressmaking or knitting pattern? If so, you will have come across some of the problems. These are caused because you do not have a chance to 'interact' with a set of instructions. You can't ask a piece of paper or a manual a question when you don't understand something!

Practise the necessary skills by trying some of the following ideas with a partner.

1. Look at the London Underground map below. Your partner must not be able to see it. Pick a starting point and describe a route to your partner. Do this once, while your partner listens but says nothing. Do it a second time, talking to each other as you go. You will soon find which is the most effective way to travel!

(Trains on the Underground are described by the direction they are going in. 'Take the Bakerloo line northbound from Waterloo and change at Oxford Circus for the Central Line westbound' is the sort of direction which makes sense.)

2. Using the London Underground map, pick a station and describe it by referring to other stations around it.

3. Use a local street map. Estate Agents may give you these if you ask nicely. Start from a place you both know. Then, by giving directions, describe a route without using street names. The objective is for both partners to end up in the same place.

4. You can stand back to back and describe actions. Try this for starters – 'I am putting the second finger on my left hand round the back of my head and holding on to my right earlobe while closing my left eye and standing on my right leg . . .'

You will find that **listening** is as important as **talking** in these exercises, and it is worth remembering that this is always the case – it is just that we sometimes forget it!

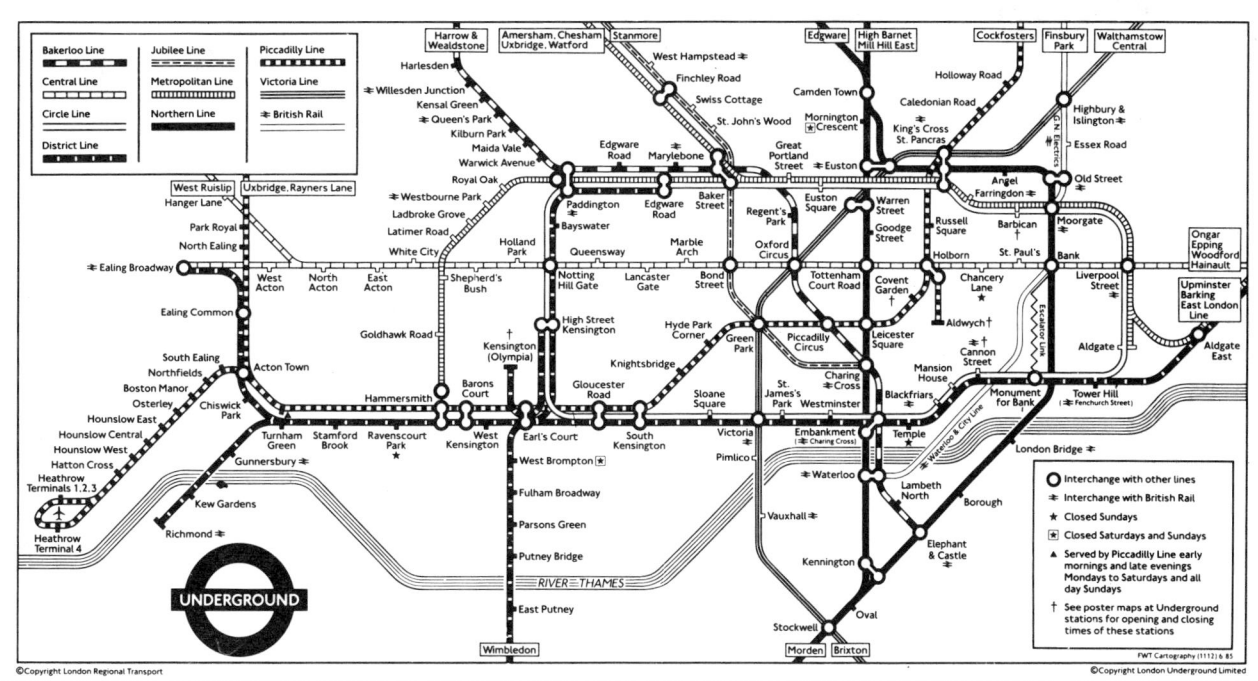

London Regional Transport Underground map   Registered user no. 87/736

EXPERT DESCRIPTION

When we describe something, we do so for all sorts of reasons. In a car accessory shop, you might hear a conversation like this . . .

Or this . . .

These are two different situations and different kinds of talk as well. The customer in the second piece might as well be on Mars for what he will understand of the first conversation.

There is an important lesson in this: we talk and listen in order to *communicate*. The best way to see this is to think of situations where one party does *not* try to communicate!

This is called 'blinding with science' and lots of people do it. Doctors are very good at it and so are officials in places like Social Security offices. In the above conversation, it was done to make the customer feel the cost was worthwhile. He is supposed to feel that a lot has been done that he could not have done himself.

It is useful to understand how 'expert' talk can be used to confuse people. But remember, as the first conversation showed, when two experts are talking, it is fast and convenient.

ARE YOU AN EXPERT TALKER?

You may be able to talk like an expert about a hobby or an interest – anything from a sport to playing the guitar. Is there someone else in the group or the class who is also an expert on the same subject? If so, try to set up some expert conversations which are expert-to-expert and deliberately make them as incomprehensible to others as possible. Then try the same talk on non-experts. See how you soon have to explain what seems obvious to you.

Look at these six pictures of old steam locomotives. Working in pairs, one of you should pick one of them and describe it to the other so that he or she can pick it out from the six.

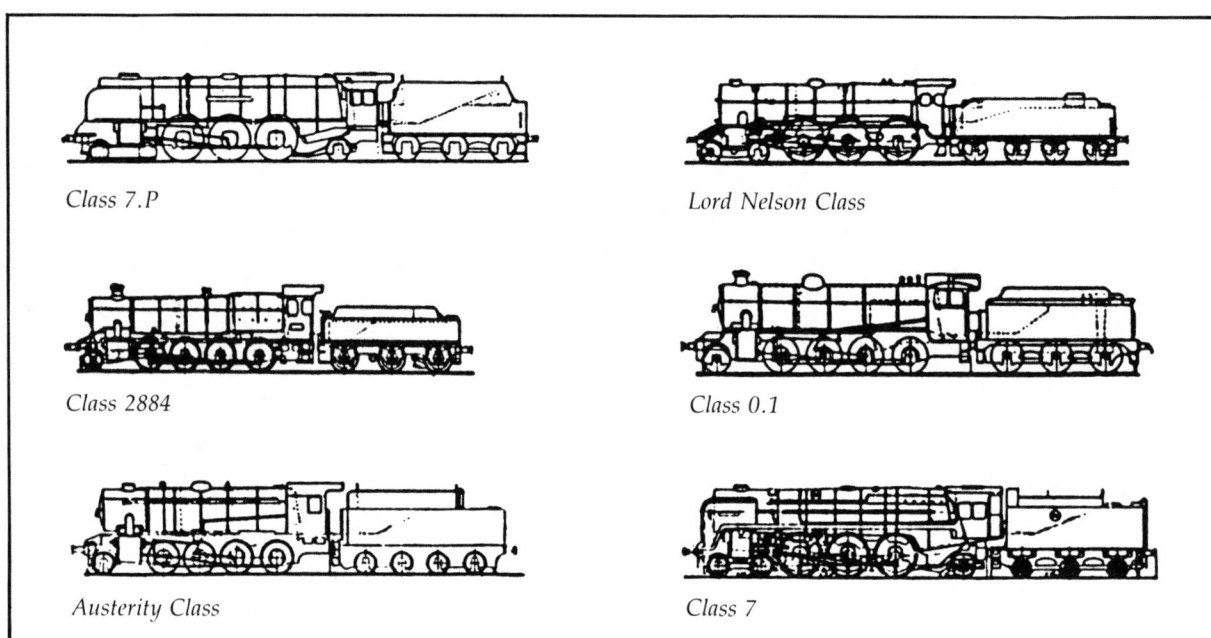

Class 7.P

Lord Nelson Class

Class 2884

Class 0.1

Austerity Class

Class 7

Now look at the diagram and see how using those terms might allow you to describe the locomotives in a different way. Because your partner has the diagram as well, you can both be very precise in what you are talking about. What would happen to the communication if the partner had no labelled diagram?

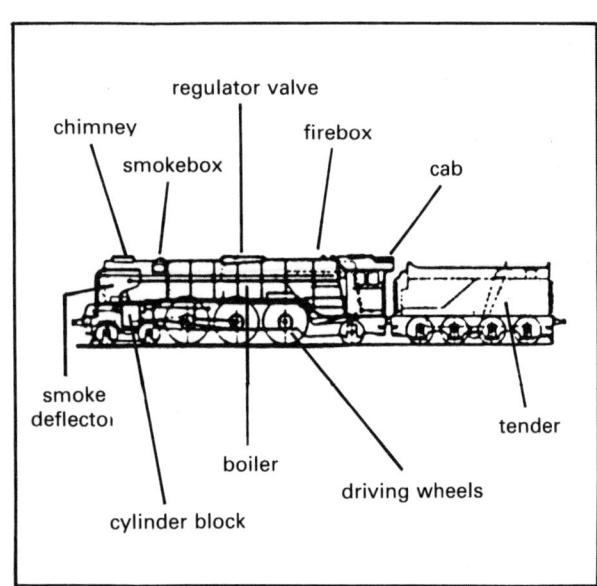

AT HOME
Find six pictures of different versions of the same things. You could try animals or natural objects like trees and flowers or cars or whatever. Old colour supplements and magazines will give you ideas. Stick the pictures onto card. You will need to find two copies of some pictures or photocopy the finished card. Use these in the same way as the locomotive pictures.

IN THE LIBRARY
Find the technical vocabulary for whatever you have chosen and produce labelled drawings to go with them. See how the description changes.

CHILD OR ADULT?

The following table gives some information about what teenagers can and cannot do at certain ages. Try covering up the right-hand column and guessing the correct age. Try asking your friends.

Get married (with parental consent)	16
Go into public houses (with parent)	14
Drink alcohol in pubs	18
Ride a motor-bike of less than 250cc	17
Buy goods on hire purchase	18
Vote in General Elections	18
Buy cigarettes	16
Serve on a jury	18
Drink wine in restaurants (with parent)	14
Leave school	16
Place a bet in a betting shop	18
Drive a car	17
Get a mortgage to buy a house	18

These raise many points you might like to discuss. Here are a few:

★ *Is there any good reason for having a different age of majority for different things?*

★ *Should there be one single age of majority at which you can do everything?*

★ *Are boys and girls treated differently in the way these laws are enforced?*

★ *Is there one thing on the list which particularly irritates you?*

Some of these questions are very *specific* and concern particular things on the list. Some are very *general* and concern the way teenagers are treated in society as a whole. To talk about them as a group will not be very constructive. You will have the familiar feeling of 'going round in circles' and 'not getting anywhere' so that your attention wanders. Perhaps two people will have an endless argument about one little thing which annoys one of them and the real issues will be ignored.

The answer is to *organise* your talk. To do that you need a chairperson. A chairperson is the person around whom all the discussion revolves. In formal meetings, everyone who speaks must talk to the chairperson rather than to each other. He or she really controls what is said. In a smaller group, the chairperson might well be doing some of the following:

★ *Introducing a new question when the discussion is getting nowhere.*

★ *Suggesting new topics for discussion.*

★ *Giving everyone a chance to put their views.*

★ *Summing up what people have said.*

★ *Bringing quiet people into the discussion.*

★ *Winding up the discussion at the end and saying what has been decided.*

Although having a chairperson makes the talk more productive, there is one problem. The chairperson must, to some extent at least, keep out of the arguments so as to keep the talk moving in the right direction. A good chairperson will not try to impose his or her views on the rest of the group.

THE TASK ▽

Hold a discussion about teenagers and the different legal age-limits for various things. One of you must act as chairperson and someone else must agree to make brief notes of what is said. It is difficult to say how long the discussion should go on. Aim for thirty minutes maximum. Tape the discussion without studying the following section, which you can then use to analyse your discussion.

WHAT HAPPENED?

Analyse the part played by the chairperson. Take a five-minute section of tape from the middle of the discussion and note down everything said by the chairperson in that time. You could make a transcript* of the section, writing down everything said. Work out in discussion:

1. For what proportion of time the chairperson was speaking.
2. The purpose of each comment he/she made. This checklist may help you:

- moved the discussion to a new point
- asked a question of someone
- gave his or her own views
- argued a point with someone
- asked someone to clarify what they meant
- stopped someone from dominating the conversation
- summarised something which had been said
- kept the discussion good-natured and friendly
- involved someone who was being quiet

A good chairperson is probably doing four or five of these things and really helping the discussion to flow and be constructive.

38

* A transcript is the written version of what has been said, with every word, hesitation and correction noted down live or from a tape-recording. It can be very useful in seeing what kind of talker you are, but it takes a long time to produce. If you want to make a transcript, perhaps for your folder, it is a good idea to keep the material you transcribe as brief as possible.

This is an extract from the transcript of a discussion about the voting age. Do you think the chairperson is doing a good job at this stage of the discussion?

Matthew: Well, you can die for your country in the ... if you're in the Army, so you should be able to vote too. Right?

Elaine: Anyway, lots of decisions ... policies have an effect on people before they're eighteen.

Gary: Yeah, changing the ... y'know, exam system and so on, er ...

Paul: More or less everything.

Gary: Yeah.

Sita: But when you're working, left school and paying taxes, then you should definitely be given the vote.

Chair: So do you think they should give people the vote when they start working, paying taxes, if that's below eighteen, sixteen or whatever?

Elaine: I think the age should be sixteen regardless.

Chair: Do people take enough interest in politics when they're sixteen?

Paul: You couldn't —

Elaine: Yes, most do ... just as much as a lot of people who <u>can</u> vote.

Paul: Well, you couldn't link the vote to working 'cos you'd disenfranchise all the unemployed.

Gary: Yeah ... What?

SEE A CHAIRPERSON AT WORK?

Local Council meetings are a good opportunity to see a chairperson at work and to understand how public meetings function. You will notice how everyone 'addresses the chair' as it is called and how the chairperson keeps quite a large number of people in order. Committee meetings with chairpeople who do not do their job properly are long-winded, never reach decisions and make people angry!

RADIO NEWS

Much of the talk which this workbook encourages you to try is discussion with plenty of time to think through your ideas. This assignment is about making what you have to say fit into very specific spaces of time. It is something which television and radio shows do all the time. Breakfast television, which looks as if people have just 'dropped in' for a chat, is actually structured to the nearest few seconds so that either the commercial break or the news comes in at exactly the right time.

THE TASK ▽

In your group, present a news summary – either television or radio – using some of the information given on page 41. You will have to:

1. Decide which items of news to use.

2. Put them in an order.

3. Re-write them.

Then:

4. Make the bulletin last EXACTLY a minute. Start with an introduction something like this:–

'On Radio Warwick it's 12.30 so now over to Wayne Wilson for the latest international, national and local news . . . '

Tape the results of this exercise and compare the summaries from different groups. How do they differ?

Now listen to a real summary using the day's newspapers and news. Is the news selected and phrased in particular ways or for a particular audience? Try taping a news summary from Radio One and comparing it with one from Radio Four on the same day.

Create your own news stories for another group to use. Make up items of news in note form and hand them to the group at the beginning of a lesson for them to create a summary. As the lesson goes on, hand them one or two additional items and up-dates on the stories so that right up to the last minute they are forced to make changes to the news summary they give.

Doing this exercise will make you conscious of how talk can be tightly controlled to fit within a given time. It may also make you think a little more about the news you hear on radio and television and about how 'what is news' is decided on. Did you know, for example, that according to some recent research the news in Britain gives more time to disasters (air crashes, train crashes, pile-ups on roads, fires etc) than almost any other news service in the world?

THE STORIES

● Bus crashed in Hampton Road this morning (517 service to Stratford-upon-Avon) in rush hour. One man detained in hospital and three passengers treated for shock. Town-centre traffic held up for over an hour.

● Trees in the area may be threatened by acid rain according to Greenpeace report published yesterday which shows that over an inch of contaminated rainfall can be expected here in any single winter month.

● Kevin and Karen Grearley, married ten days ago, returned from honeymoon in Majorca to their new home, on Shakespeare Avenue, to find it severely damaged by vandals. Doors broken down, furniture damaged and graffiti on walls. Mr Grearley (father of husband) is disgusted.

● Triumph Motor Company announce the launch today of a new car – the Triumph Bermuda. It has a Japanese engine and German gearbox. Designed to appeal to executive market.

● Saudi Arabian Airlines Boeing 747 has been hi-jacked shortly after leaving Jeddah. Hi-jackers demanding release of four-teen members of the Blue Buttonhole Revolutionary Party. Have threatened to blow up plane if no re-sponse by end of day.

● The Prime Minister is to visit the area in three months' time to open the new Social Security buildings in Leamington Spa.

* * * * * * LATE NEWS * * * * * *

● The hi-jacked jet has landed in Southern India and is now surrounded by Indian troops and police. Negotiations with the hi-jackers are believed to be taking place.

THE BOOK PROGRAMME

This assignment is a more complex version of Assignment 17, **Radio News**. It simulates a TV programme about books and reading. Again, what you are trying to do is to work as a team and to produce something which fits into a precise time-schedule. It is important that the programme is interesting and that probably means that it must be varied.

THE TASK ▽

Your brief is to make a twenty-minute edition of a programme called 'Books for Everyone' which is particularly about teenage reading. Start with a group discussion and decide who will take on which roles. You will need a producer, a script-writer, some presenters, and interviewers. It is up to you to decide what should be in your programme but some of the following suggestions might help your first discussions:

★ *An interview with someone about their favourite books*

★ *Some book reviews*

★ *A discussion about violence in teenage fiction*

★ *A discussion about ways to improve the school library*

These are just ideas. It's up to your group to think up others and to organise them into a continuous presentation which is properly introduced, carefully linked and smooth-running.

Aim to have two or three meetings to work on the material. The first meeting will be about what you think you might include. Then, singly or in pairs, do any necessary research. At your second meeting you should have material to read and discuss. Decide what to cut out or where there are gaps. The third meeting can be your final run-through. Think about producing titles, credits, adding theme music and getting the timing right at this stage.

If you have video facilities available, try to tape this assignment. It will tell you a lot about your ability to 'project' your personality. If you have time, work on this aspect in particular. And remember that you don't have to be beautiful to be a success on TV! It is just a matter of making the impression that you are a pleasant, lively person. Viewers actually watch faces and hands for the clues which give these impressions. Make sure you use yours!

A FORMAL DEBATE

A formal debate is a peculiar (and polite) way of having an argument. It has a **motion**, which is what is discussed, and **proposers** and **opposers** who argue for and against the motion. The main place in this country where you will see or hear debates is in the House of Commons, where Members of Parliament insult each other in the nicest possible way! Courts operate in a very similar way except that the motion is about whether someone is guilty of an offence and the proposers and opposers are replaced by the prosecution and the defence.

In thinking of a title for a debate, make sure that it is something about which you know something or about which you can find out something. Using evidence is one of the most important things to be able to do. Also, it is useful to have a subject about which you genuinely disagree.

The title of a debate is always expressed as a statement which begins **'This House believes that . . . '.** Of course, if you don't believe that, then you are opposing the motion!

Here are some possible titles–

THIS HOUSE BELIEVES THAT:

'there should be advertising on BBC TV and radio.'

'Sixth-formers should all be in colleges not in schools.'

'there should be no new nuclear power stations built in the United Kingdom.'

'eating meat is wrong.'

What matters is the *quality* of the argument which you put forward and not the motion. If you are proposing a motion, then *all* the points you make must be in favour of it and you must be determined to see your motion passed.

Assignments 11, 12 and 13 will have given you some clues as to how to plan your speech.

Debates are a bit different in that you normally have a **seconder** to support what the first speaker says and also a chance for the proposer to come back and deal with the arguments put forward by the opposition. It sounds complicated but it isn't really. Look at the outline of a typical debate below.

A TYPICAL DEBATE

1. The chairperson speaks first to say what the motion is and to introduce the speakers.

2. The proposer defines and supports the motion, speaking for four or five minutes.

3. The opposer speaks for the same length of time. One of his or her duties is to argue against some of the points which have just been made.

4. The seconder for the motion speaks for less time (perhaps three minutes). He/She brings in additional arguments as well as arguing against what has just been said by the opposer.

5. The seconder for the opposition does the same.

6. The opposer then sums up the opposition's views and argues against what has been heard from the proposition. Summing up might take two minutes.

7. The proposer now speaks again, dealing with arguments raised and urging the audience to support the motion.

8. Finally, the chairperson asks the audience (or **floor** as they are called) to make points of their own.

9. After this general discussion, a vote can be taken and the motion 'won' or 'lost'.

Just how rigidly you stick to this outline is a matter of personal choice. Many teachers expect the timing to be exact so that, as you speak, you receive a warning (classroom lights flashed on) when there are thirty seconds of your time left. At the end of your time, the lights come on and you must stop.

What is good about debating like this, is that you must deal with the arguments which you have just heard, rather than give a prepared speech. A really good debater will turn your arguments against you and make them seem trivial and unimportant. You will have to respond quickly. 'Thinking on your feet' is hard at first. But it will give you confidence in any situation, in later life, where you have to speak out.

'Let me take up the point Emma made just now...'

A GROUP RESEARCH PROJECT

I hope this book has encouraged you to think about the way you talk and about how to take part in discussions. On the way, you have been asked to think about your own performance as a talker and to help to assess the talk of your friends. In this final assignment, you are given the chance to look at and analyse the ways in which other people use talk, by carrying out your own research project. This not only involves watching others talking but also taking all sorts of decisions, and talking them through, on the way!

There are a number of features of talk which are well worth looking at in this way. You can investigate any one of these areas or another of your choice.

All the activities need a discussion group for you to study, and a topic for them to use as a starting point for the discussion. It is vital that your subjects do not know *what* you are studying because if they are aware of what you are looking for, they will behave in an unnatural way. It might make most sense to use a group from a lower year and to 'borrow' them from another lesson. You will get the best results if you keep calm, reassure your subject group and set up a peaceful and relaxed environment for the experiment.

1. **The difference between the ways in which boys and girls contribute to group discussions**

   Did you know that, in a discussion between a mixed group, boys talk far more than girls? They also interrupt each other more than girls do. But boys are even more likely to interrupt girls than other boys. Sometimes, if a girl is speaking, boys will not pay attention but if a boy speaks they will listen. If a girl speaks up and says her fair share, boys will often tell her she is talking too much. Think of all the jokes you have heard about the way women 'gossip', 'chat' and 'natter' all day. Well, research suggests that it just isn't true that women talk more than men – even at work, men talk more.

   To look at this area, you will obviously need a mixed group and a topic which both boys and girls find interesting. Then, record the sort of contribution each person makes to the discussion. Record whether they stated something, or moved the conversation along by asking a question or saying, 'Go on,' for example. (These sorts of contribution can be listed under the two simple headings *Made statement* and *Asked question*.) Record each interruption too, and the sexes of both the interrupter and the speaker.

   The best way to do this is for each person in your group to 'shadow' one of the experimental group. They sit behind their partners and fill in a sheet laid out something like this:

Name of subject	Sex (m or f)	Made statement (tick)	Asked question (tick)	Interrupted (m or f)	Was interrupted (by m or f)
Lucy Smith	F	✓✓✓	✓	F M	M F
Mark Brown	M	✓✓	✓✓	F	M F F

2. **The differences between talk and writing – Meta-language**

One big difference between talk and writing is what is called by some people *meta-language*. These are the bits and pieces of words which we use, like oil in an engine, to lubricate talk and to make it run smoothly but they don't have any content or say anything new. When someone says, 'Can I get a word in now?', 'What we mean then is . . . ', 'Stick to the point!' or 'I'll say it again . . . ' they are using meta-language to request the right to speak, to summarise the discussion so far, to define the subject more closely or to emphasise a point. With a transcript of part of a taped discussion, you could analyse the meta-language used by successful talkers. Of course, if you can use this kind of language, it is likely that your voice is the one which will be heard! You could relate this to a look at what makes a dominant talker dominate a conversation. Everyone has met people like this. They are 'loudmouthed' in discussion and might not let you get a word in edgeways, but when you want

someone to speak on your behalf, for instance to explain to the P.E. teacher that it really is too cold for you to go outside, then they can turn out to be quite useful! If you have a dominating speaker in your group, look at how he or she controls the group.

3. **The differences between talk and writing – How body language works**

A video will help enormously in studying this but it is possible to do without. Set up an argument. Choose a subject you can be sure will cause disagreement. Set two pairs to argue the case. Tape the discussion and draw the positions of the group like 'stick men', noting particularly their arms, hands, legs and the angle of the head. Every time they move position, do a new drawing to show which arm or leg has shifted and note the time. (You will need one person to do this for each of the four people being observed but don't do a whole new drawing each time – just draw the bit which has moved!)

Watching Simon (he is sitting down)

Times	Position	Detail	Body language
0 mins		arms folded	rather defensive
2 mins		R hand raised to chin	showing interest?
4 mins		hd. slanted legs crossed	makes contribution (shyly)
6 mins		hd. up hands used expressively	making a point/ getting involved
10 mins		arms folded distracted to R	getting bored

Afterwards you can compare the drawings and the tape to see how each pair arguing may take up similar positions or both move together. They may also become more 'aggressive' to make a particular point or even more 'submissive' if the argument is going against them. Of course, it is very important that they do not know what you are doing or their gestures will be very self-conscious.

Having worked through these assignments, you will have realised that much of the talk we use in our day-to-day lives is to solve problems or to help us complete particular tasks and jobs more effectively. Reading through the newspapers could give you some topical ideas or, if you are really stuck, you could modify one of the other assignments in this book. Don't take part in the discussion you set up – your job is to observe. Ideally, you could video what takes place or make an audio tape.

When you have finished this assignment, write a report to explain what you did and to present your findings to the rest of the group.

n. **O'racy,** skill in self-expression and ability to communicate freely with others by word of mouth

Chambers Twentieth Century Dictionary